About This Book

Out & About Math is the perfect resource to help your students make the connection between the math skills they learn in the classroom and their real-life applications. Packed with loads of thematic fun, each activity helps teach national math standards in a developmentally appropriate way.

Out & About Math contains nine curriculum-based teaching units. Each unit features a different real-life location, such as the playground, the grocery store, or the ice-cream shop. To bring the feel of the featured location into the classroom, most units begin with directions for setting up a center area that replicates the location. The various hands-on activities can then be completed by students visiting the center. The activities within each unit are designed to "pull out" the math that would naturally occur in the featured location. Specific skills are listed at the beginning of each activity, so you'll quickly know which skills are being reinforced. Each unit contains student reproducibles and/or pattern pages used in conjunction with the activities. The *Out & About Math* activities are designed to encourage your students to use higher-level thinking and problem-solving skills with real-life applications.

What Is Real-Life Math?

Traditionally, students have been taught *how* to do math but not *why* they are doing math. In one of its fact sheets on mathematics education, the NCTM (National Council of Teachers of Mathematics) states, "...mathematics must entail the study, understanding, and application of a set of concepts and skills commonly used by real people, in real settings, every day." Math in the real world isn't a row of math problems to solve. Instead, real-life math involves bringing together an array of skills in order to solve daily problems, answer questions, plan tasks, or gather and interpret data. Textbook math often involves contrived, single-step problems for which there is one correct answer. Real-life problems, on the other hand, occur naturally and often require multiple steps. A person has to decide which procedure(s) to use to solve a real-life problem. Sometimes there is missing data in a real-life problem that has to be collected in order to solve the problem. Sometimes a real-world problem can have more than one answer as well as more than one strategy for achieving the answer. Thinking mathematically and then applying this knowledge to everyday situations is very empowering for students. The activities in *Out & About Math* help students develop their mathematical thinking skills as well as develop an appreciation for math in their everyday lives.

How to Use This Book

Out & About Math is designed to be flexible to help you meet the needs of your students as well as your needs as a teacher. Since it's not feasible to take students to each location, most units begin with directions for setting up a center area in your classroom to replicate the location (see the center setup below). This allows students to recall prior experiences in similar situations and apply that knowledge to various hands-on activities. Activities can also be done independently of the center setup. The pick-and-choose nature of the activities allows you to select just the right ones to complete with your students, whether you're setting up a center area or using the activities with small groups of students. To help you even more, skill lines have been included just below each activity title so that you can quickly determine the skills addressed in each activity. We've also provided a handy organizer (pages 4–5) that lists all the skills covered in the book and in which units the activities featuring each skill can be found.

Table of Contents

National Standard	Skill	Playground	Grocery Store	Post Office	Movie Theater	Farm	Ice-Cream Parlor	Pizza Place	Garden Center	Ballpark
Number and Operations	addition				●	●			●	●
	counting	●	●	●	●	●	●	●	●	●
	matching numerals			●		●				
	number order									●
	number recognition	●	●	●	●					
	one-to-one correspondence			●		●		●		
	following a sequence							●		
	sequencing							●		
	sequencing ordinal numbers	●					●			●
	set, numeral, and number matching								●	
	subtraction						●			
	writing numbers				●					
Algebra	categorizing		●							
	classifying							●		
	patterns	●	●							
	sorting	●		●		●	●		●	
	sorting by attributes	●	●			●				
Measurement	coin recognition		●	●			●		●	●
	coin value		●	●	●		●			●
	using money			●	●	●			●	
	comparing amounts	●				●			●	
	comparing sets		●				●	●	●	
	comparing size			●						
	comparing volume					●				
	comparing weight		●							
	estimating amounts					●	●		●	
	estimating time						●	●		●
	estimating volume					●			●	
	estimating weight			●					●	
	measuring time						●	●		●
	measuring volume					●			●	
	measuring weight			●		●			●	
	nonstandard measurement	●							●	
	size seriation					●			●	
	time to the hour				●	●				●
	understanding concepts of time				●					
Geometry	comparing sizes and shapes of plane figures					●				
	identifying shapes	●	●					●		
Data Analysis and Probability	gathering information	●								
	graphing	●		●	●				●	
	recording information	●								
	surveying						●	●		
	tallying				●	●	●			●

Out & About at the Playground

These math activities are perfect for any playground environment, whether it's a paved schoolyard, an indoor gym, a rural field, or a modern park with the latest equipment. Pick and choose from what's available to you and adapt these ideas as desired. Then take your class out to play. It's time for math! All set? Let's go!

Copy Me
Skill: copying and extending patterns

Here's a pleasing pattern game for the playground or indoors! To prepare, duplicate the pattern cards (page 11) onto tagboard to make a supply. Cut the cards apart; then laminate them for durability if desired. Gather students and show them a simple pattern made from the cards. Demonstrate the pattern; then repeat with students copying your movements.

When youngsters have the hang of it, encourage them to continue the pattern after the cards run out. Invite a volunteer to create a pattern for the rest of the group to copy. Continue in this manner until all interested volunteers have had a turn. To vary this activity, take students to the playground and have them find patterns in their play, such as swings moving back and forth and sliders moving up and down.

Sort It Out
Skill: sorting by attributes

Here's a sorting activity that combines attributes with playground fun. Gather a chart tablet and marker; then take your students to the playground. Slowly give clues that describe a particular piece of equipment or an activity on your playground, such as "You can slide on this piece." Have students think of the activity as it's described. Then encourage each child to go to the activity described when she knows the answer. Continue to describe the activity until it's apparent to all students. Discuss and record the name of the activity and the clues that made it clear to the majority of students. For more challenge, describe the equipment or activities with more difficult attributes, such as color, shape, or material.

Slide
- You can slide on this piece.
- It has a ladder.
- One person can slide at a time.
- You sit on this and slide to the bottom.
- It's black and blue.

Playground Photo Math

Skills: counting, sorting, comparing amounts

Picture the math possibilities in this activity! Take photos of your youngsters playing on the playground. Be sure to capture varying numbers of students in the photos. Include one photo of a piece of equipment with no children. If desired, mount the photos on index cards and laminate them for durability. During a small-group time, encourage students to count and compare the number of children pictured in each photo. Invite students to sort the pictures by number of children and use the phrases *more*, *equal*, and *fewer than* to describe them.

Picture-Perfect Shapes

Skills: identifying shapes, sorting

Don't put away that camera yet! Use it to capture some playground shapes for ongoing learning. Obtain a supply of brightly colored sticky dots. Take youngsters to the playground and show them how to find a shape in the environment, such as a triangle in the slide. Demonstrate marking the shape with sticky dots. Next, divide your class into small groups and give each group a set of dots. Send each group to a different area of the playground to search for and mark shapes. Circulate among the groups confirming and photographing the found shapes. Gather students and have each group share the shapes it found. Later, photocopy sets of the pictures using a marker to enlarge the dots as needed and store them in a center. Encourage students in this center to use a crayon to trace the marked shapes on a copy.

Heel to Toe

Skills: nonstandard measurement, counting, recording information

Just how many steps does it take to get from the slide to the swing? This activity will have your youngsters measuring in no time! To prepare, create a simple recording sheet similar to the one shown, depicting your playground's equipment or layout. Duplicate the sheet for each group of three students. Also prepare the playground for this activity by making lines (with tape, chalk, or flour) to match the recording sheet. Gather your class around one line and demonstrate how to carefully step heel to toe to measure distance in footsteps; then count aloud the steps and record the number on the sheet. Divide the students into groups of three and give each group a recording sheet and crayon. Help each group find a different line and then begin measuring with one student stepping, one counting the steps aloud, and one recording the final number. Next, have the groups rotate to a new line, change roles within their group, and measure and record the distance. Continue in this manner until each group completes its recording sheet. So how many steps does it take to get from the slide to the swing?

How Many Steps?	
Measure From Piece to Piece	Steps
slide to swing	20
swing to sandbox	
door to sandbox	
beam to slide	
bench to swing	
beam to hopscotch	
bench to sandbox	

We Like to Play!

swing	slide	beam	balls	hopscotch	sandbox	climbing	racing
Beth	Tom	Kim	Lenny	Nancy	Jesse	Luna	Sam
Kyle	Manu		Dave	Gabbie	Heidi	Sofia	Blake
D'Angelo	Carole		Bill				
Vinny							

The Best Part Is...

Skills: graphing, counting

Try this great graph to turn recess into meaningful math. To prepare, use a permanent marker to draw on an old shower curtain or vinyl tablecloth a large grid sized to accommodate your class. Make a set of blank cards sized to fit within each cell. Have each child write her name on a card, and reserve the rest to label the graph columns with your playground's equipment and activities. Also make a card to title the graph as shown. Store the graph, cards, a roll of tape, and a marker in a basket. Then take the basket outside during recess.

At the end of your designated playtime, spread the graph on the ground and gather your students around. Invite students to share their favorite playground equipment and activities as you program a different blank card for each. Tape each card to the top of a different column and then pass out the children's name cards. Call out the first activity choice and ask each child who prefers it to place his card in that column. Continue in this manner until the graph is complete; then discuss and compare the results. So how many more children prefer the swing than the slide?

Pick a Number
***Skills:** number recognition, counting*

Coordinating play with numeral recognition and counting is a cinch with this activity! In advance, make a color-coordinated chart, similar to the one shown, of some of your playground equipment. Cut a supply of matching color paper squares; then program each with a numeral from 1 to 20. Store them in a paper bag. Pair your students and take them, the chart, and the bag to the playground.

Show students the chart and point out the colors. Next, demonstrate how to match a color square with the activity, read aloud the number, and then perform the activity the number of times indicated. Have one child from each pair choose a square, match it with the activity, and then perform the activity the number of times indicated while his partner counts aloud. Have the partners switch roles and then trade the square for another from the bag. Continue until most pairs have had turns at each activity or until interest wanes. Wow—18 ball bounces and six trips down the slide! That's a lot of counting!

Time to Move On
***Skill:** sequencing ordinal numbers*

Orderly play takes on a new meaning with this activity! In advance, sketch or take photos of six playground activities. Photocopy the pictures; then use them to prepare a different lotto-style card for each small group of students. Number the pictured activities 1–6 as shown. Recruit six older student volunteers, one to stand at each of the six activity stations with a crayon.

To complete the activity, discuss with your class ordinal numbers for numerals 1–6. Take students to the playground and divide them into six groups. Next, give a card to each group. Explain that each group uses ordinal numbers to tell the volunteer at each station the group's playing order. Have each volunteer compare the group's statement to its card, and, if correct, check off that station and invite the group to play. If incorrect, the volunteer sends the group to find its correct station. After a designated time, signal the groups to move to their next station. Continue in this fashion until each group has completed its card; then gather the students. Invite children to compare and discuss their cards using ordinal numbers.

We're playing here fourth!

Name _____

Playground Picks

Ask each family member what his or her favorite playground activity is. Make a tally in the circle that matches it below.

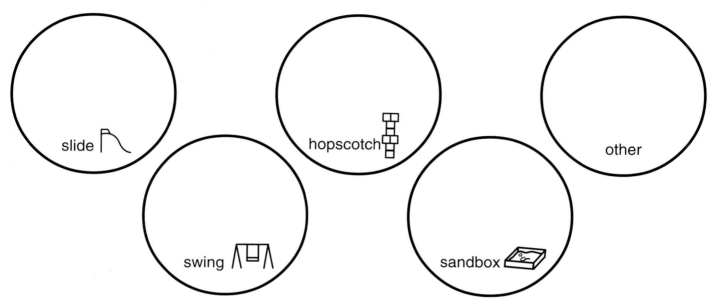

Color one graph box for each tally mark.

My Family Likes to Play!

5					
4					
3					
2					
1					
	slide	swing	hopscotch	sandbox	other

Type of Activity

What is the favorite playground activity? _____

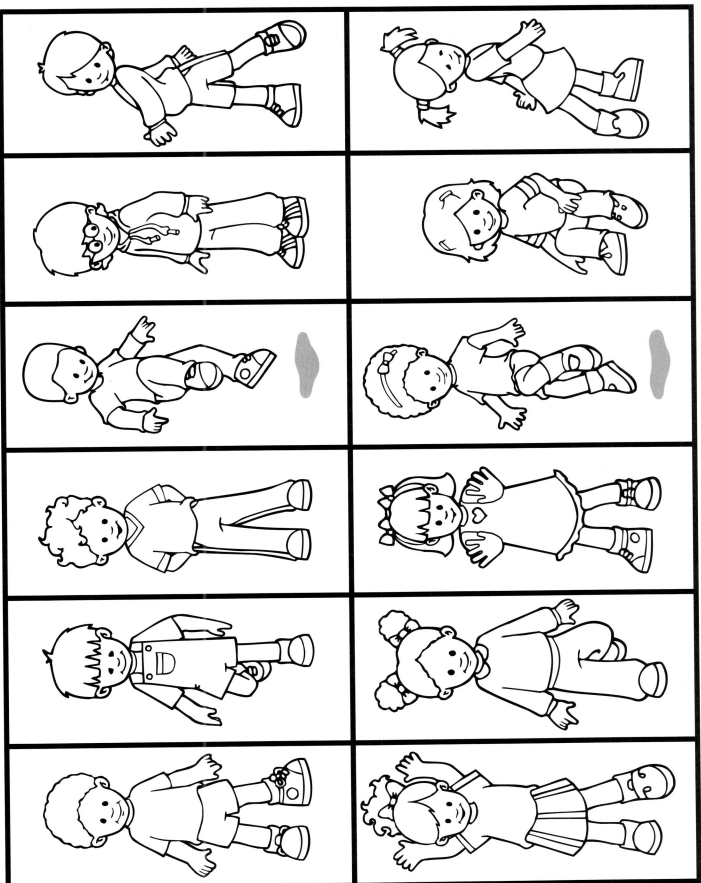

Out & About at the Grocery Store

These math activities make a wonderful weekly special! Math abounds in grocery stores all over the world, with lots of weighing, counting, measuring, and money exchanging. Take your little ones shopping for some tasty bargains when you simulate a store in your classroom. Prepare a center by stocking shelves with plastic play foods and a variety of clean, empty boxes and plastic containers from real foods such as cereals, crackers, fruit snacks, juice, milk, eggs, and yogurt. If desired, create separate sections for baked goods, meats (cut from craft foam), produce, and refrigerated foods as found in a real store. Create a checkout with paper bags, a low table, and a sturdy flat box decorated to resemble a cash register. (Fill the register with copies of the coin patterns on page 63.) Add extra touches of realism with shopping baskets, coupons, and pencils and paper for lists. If possible, place this center near the home-living center so students can pretend to take the groceries home and use them.

To strengthen the connection to real life, invite a local grocer to speak to your class. If desired, plan a field trip to a nearby grocery store. Take along a list of a few snack foods to purchase and then serve at school. Encourage parents to take their children with them on a trip to the grocery store during this study. All set? Let's go!

Hot Now!

*Skills: **identifying shapes, number recognition, counting***

Fresh and delicious pastries, cookies, croissants, and cakes are some of the tempting treats available in the grocery bakery. These delicacies have distinctive shapes, so they're just right for shape-reinforcement practice during dramatic play. To prepare this center, make a supply of the patterns on page 16 and then mount them onto cardboard or foam core. Cut out the shapes; then decorate each to resemble that type of baked good. Display the goods on cookie sheets (or sheets of gray construction paper) on a tabletop. Place a spatula nearby. Also make a supply of the order forms on page 17; then store them in the center along with a pencil, paper lunch bags, and an apron for the baker.

Invite a pair of children at this center to take turns playing a baker and a customer. Instruct the customer to examine the baked goods and place an order by marking the number of each desired shape on an order form. Have her hand it to the baker, who will then use the spatula to transfer the order to a paper bag. Encourage both students to count aloud and name the shapes as the order is filled. For more challenge, add prices to the order form, provide the customer with a filled coin purse, and have her purchase her treats. Tasty!

Plenty of Produce

Skills: counting, sorting by attributes, comparing sets

Mmm—plenty of fresh fruits and veggies are found in the produce aisle. Send your little shoppers out to pick the best produce around. To prepare, place on a table a variety of plastic fruits and vegetables (or cut the items from craft foam). Number a set of cards from 0 to 10 and store it in a basket nearby. Place several paper lunch bags near the produce. To use this center, a child takes a number and then picks that many fruits and vegetables to place in his bag. Challenge each child to then unpack his produce onto the floor and sort it by different attributes such as green/not green, stem/no stem, and bumpy/not bumpy. Discuss the sorted produce with the child and encourage him to compare the groups using the terms *more, fewer than,* and *equal.*

"Cent-sible" Savings

Skills: coin recognition, coin value

Planning ahead will help save your little shoppers some money during this activity! In advance, make a supply of the sales flyer on page 18. Also gather a quantity of play coins (or duplicate the pattern on page 63 to make a supply). Place the flyers at the entrance to the grocery store center; then make sure there are several empty containers of each featured item shelved in the center. Pass out a penny, nickel, dime, and quarter to each child in a small group. Have each child pick up a flyer; then explain how to use it to find bargains. Invite him to plan how to best spend all his money and then begin shopping with his coins. Play the role of cashier and take his coins in exchange for the featured products. When each child has spent his money, gather the group to discuss coin value and the different combinations of choices. Wow—what super bargains!

Balancing Act
Skill: *comparing weight*

Weighing items is a familiar part of many visits to the grocery store. Discuss with students items that are regularly sold by weight, such as produce, baked goods, coffee, and meats. To prepare, place a balance scale and a food portion scale or postal scale in a center. Add some fresh fruits and veggies such as apples and carrots and other weighed items such as bulk foods, flour, oatmeal, and sugar. Also include some paper and pencils. Then send pairs of students to the grocery store center to weigh some items for themselves. Invite each pair to select two items to weigh and compare. Have the students estimate which item is heavier and then place both items on the balance scale and record their findings. Have the pair weigh and compare three or four pairs of items. For more weighing practice, have each student take a turn weighing an item on the other scale.

Mix-Up in Aisle One!
Skill: *categorizing*

Here's a three-player Go Fish–style game to encourage cooperation while reinforcing categorization skills. In advance, fill each of three paper grocery bags with a variety of clean, empty food containers and play food. Explain to the players that someone didn't follow his shopping list and bought the wrong foods. They have to straighten out the mess and take the correct foods home. Next, stand the players in a triangle, give each a bag, and assign each one a storage category—freezer, pantry, or refrigerator. Have Player 1 ask Player 2 if she has any foods in her assigned category; then have that child search in her bag for one item in that category. If she has one, she gives it to Player 1 and then asks Player 3 for a food in her category. Play continues in this manner as students search their groceries for the foods they need. The game is over when all the foods are sorted into the correct bags. For more challenge, encourage each player to ask for specific foods in his category, such as frozen peas or ice cream.

Name _____

Favorite Foods

 Color.

 Cut.

Glue to finish the pattern.

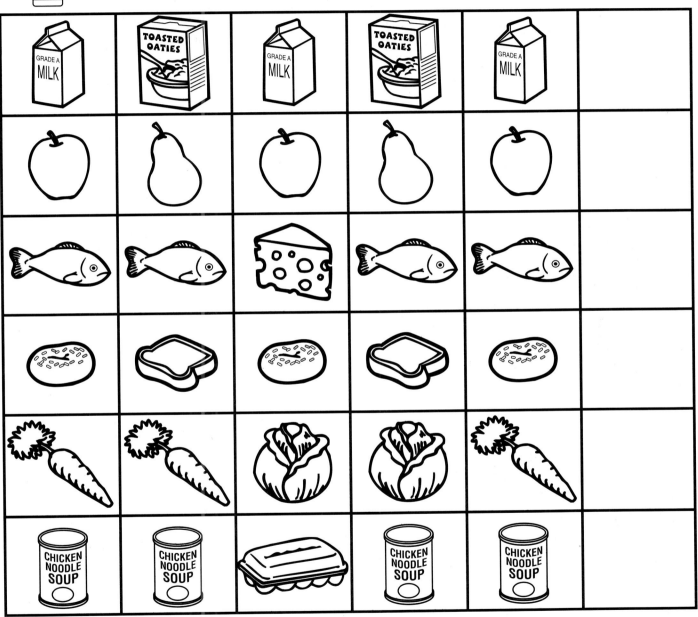

Baked Goods Patterns
Use with "Hot Now!" on page 12.

Bakery Treats

brownie

cupcake

cookie

pie

danish

croissant

roll

©The Education Center, Inc. • *Out & About Math* • TEC3079

Bakery Treats

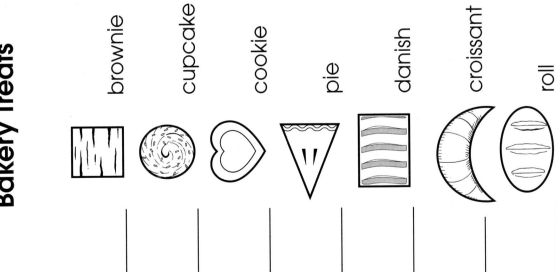

brownie

cupcake

cookie

pie

danish

croissant

roll

©The Education Center, Inc. • *Out & About Math* • TEC3079

Flyer
Use with " 'Cent-sible' Savings" on page 13.

Weekly Specials

eggs

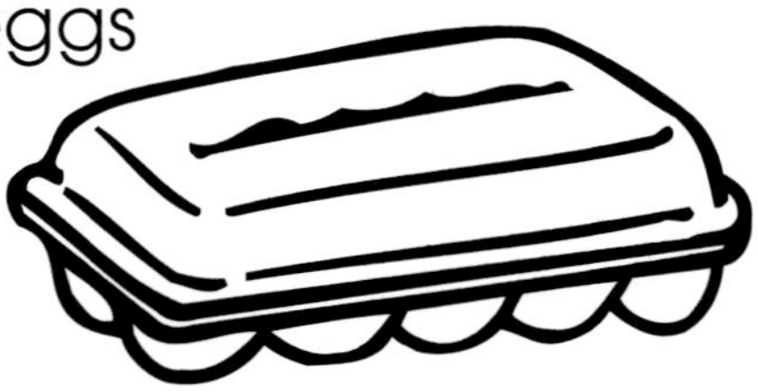

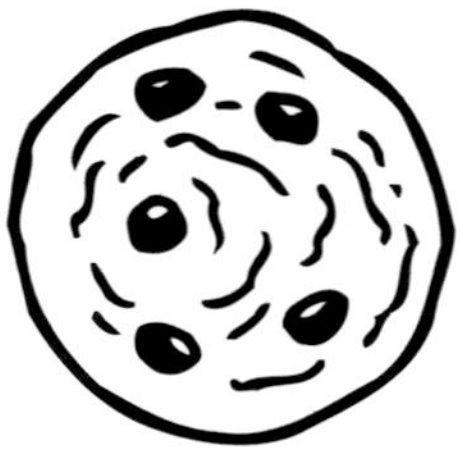

cookie

juice box

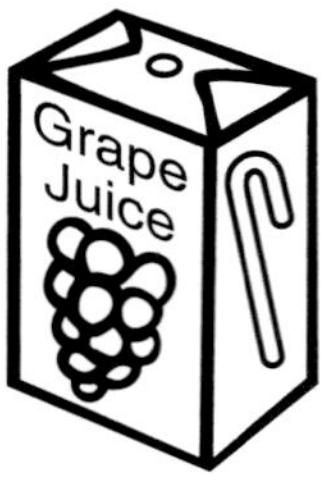

Grape
Juice

1¢

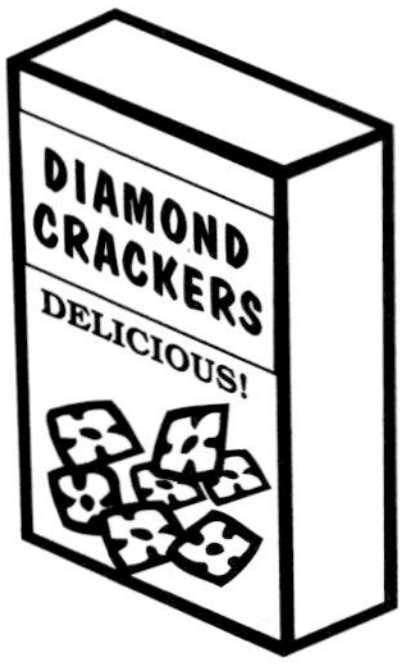

DIAMOND
CRACKERS
DELICIOUS!

crackers

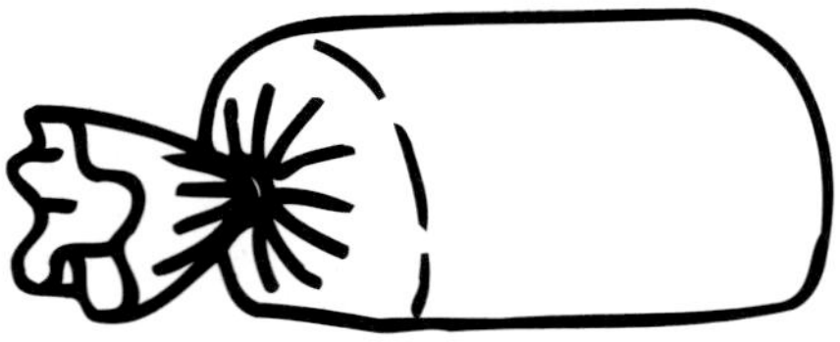

bread

5¢

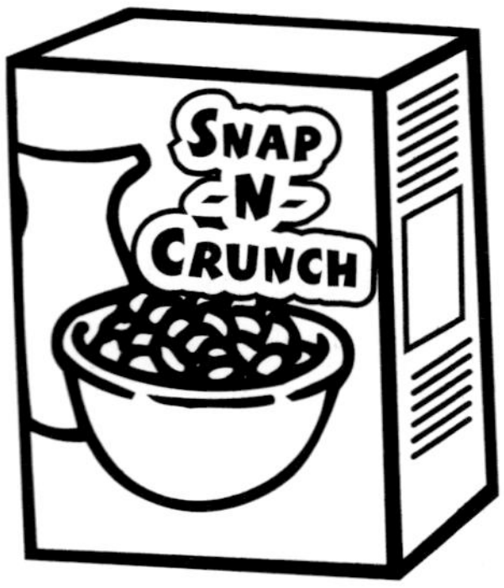

SNAP
N
CRUNCH

cereal

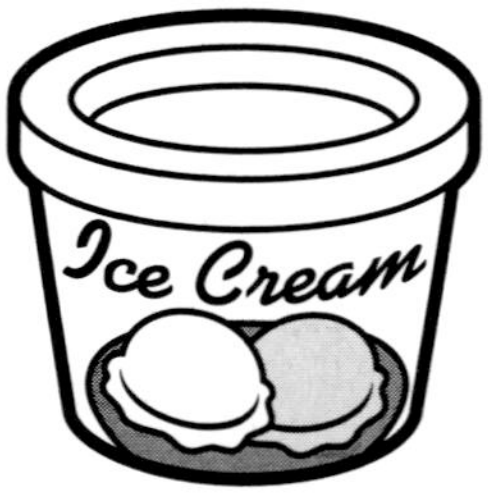

Ice Cream

ice cream

10¢

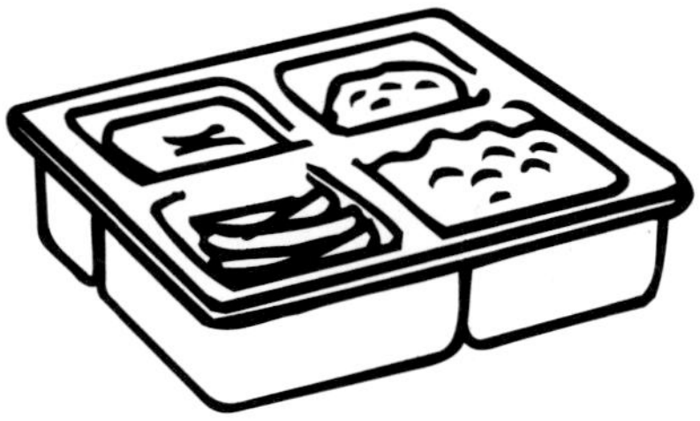

lunch tray

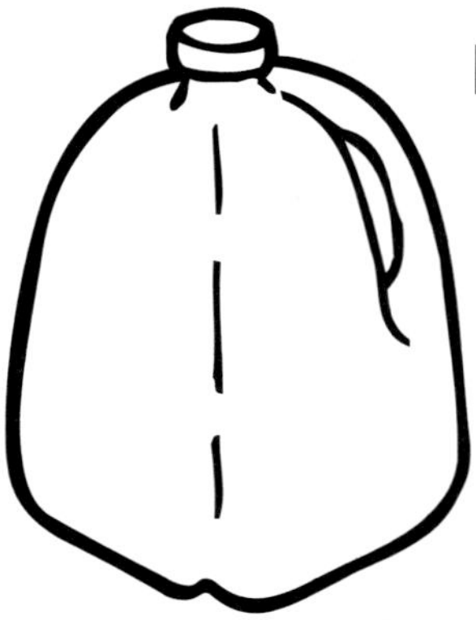

milk

25¢

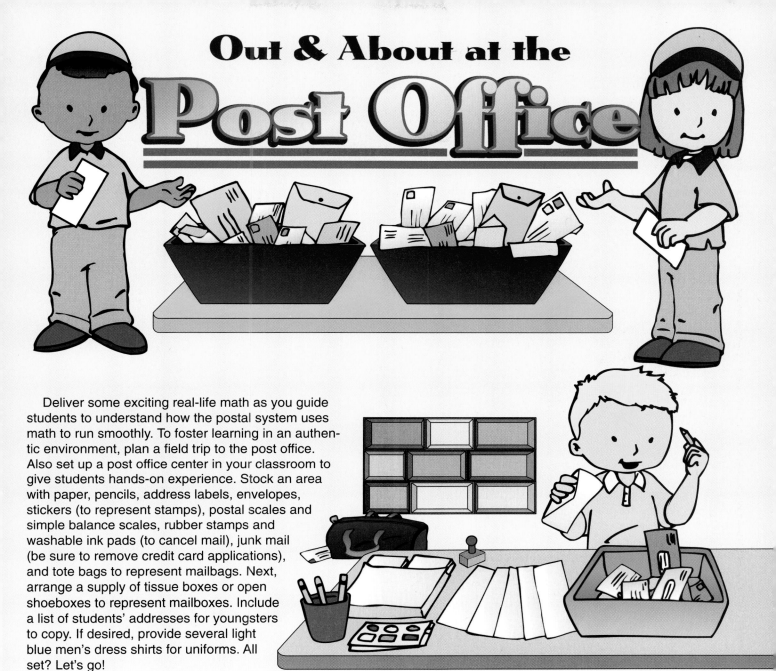

Out & About at the Post Office

Deliver some exciting real-life math as you guide students to understand how the postal system uses math to run smoothly. To foster learning in an authentic environment, plan a field trip to the post office. Also set up a post office center in your classroom to give students hands-on experience. Stock an area with paper, pencils, address labels, envelopes, stickers (to represent stamps), postal scales and simple balance scales, rubber stamps and washable ink pads (to cancel mail), junk mail (be sure to remove credit card applications), and tote bags to represent mailbags. Next, arrange a supply of tissue boxes or open shoeboxes to represent mailboxes. Include a list of students' addresses for youngsters to copy. If desired, provide several light blue men's dress shirts for uniforms. All set? Let's go!

3 Club St.
Durham, NC

4 Club St.
Durham, NC

5 Club St.
Durham, NC

6 Club St.
Durham, NC

4 Club St.
Durham, NC

6 Club St.
Durham, NC

Special Delivery
Skills: sorting, matching numerals

Begin your post office study with this inviting center activity! In advance, address a set of manila envelopes with the same street name, but different house numbers from 0 to 20. Also address a matching set of blank postcards (or index cards) and then store them in a mailbag. Attach the open envelopes to a bulletin board or wall within easy student reach and place the mailbag nearby. To use this center, a student removes a card from the mailbag, reads the address, and places it in the matching envelope. He continues in this manner until all the mail is delivered. Hey, this one's for you.

Stamp Champs

Skills: number recognition, one-to-one correspondence, counting

Here's a fun center-time game for some skill-building dramatic play. In advance, duplicate a large supply of the stamp and envelope patterns on page 24. Cut out the pieces and store them in the center along with a couple of glue sticks and a set of cards labeled with numerals 1–10. Before opening the center, explain to your class that stamps are used to pay for the letter's delivery and that postal workers cancel stamps to ensure that each one is only used once. Next, demonstrate how to check for the stamp in the upper right corner of the envelope and then mark over it with a rubber stamp so it can't be used again.

Select a pair of volunteers (a customer and postal worker) to visit the center. To play, the customer chooses a number card, reads the numeral aloud, and then glues one stamp each to that many envelopes. Have the customer mail his letters by giving them to the postal worker. The postal worker checks his work by using a rubber stamp to cancel the same number of stamped envelopes. Have the students switch roles and repeat for several turns.

Postal Practice

Skill: coin recognition, coin values

There's a lot of money changing hands at the post office, so provide youngsters with some hands-on practice in your classroom post office! Program a copy of the stamp patterns (page 24) with coin values and then duplicate to make a supply. Post one copy as a price list. Then cut apart the remaining copies and store the stamps in the center. Also include a supply of envelopes (or copies of the pattern on page 24), a cash register (box), and several coin purses filled with play money (use copies of the coin patterns on page 63) or real coins, if desired. Explain to your class that stamps have different prices, depending on how much postage they represent. Next, show students a variety of stamps, including postcard and first-class stamps, and point out where each value is marked. Demonstrate how to purchase a stamp from a postal worker, affix it to an envelope, and then mail it. For independent practice, have visitors in the post office center take turns pretending to be the postal worker and customer so everyone has a chance to buy and sell.

Time to Weigh!

Skills: *estimating and measuring weight, comparing size*

Postal workers must carefully weigh packages for shipping. Use this activity to package measurement and comparison skills! Obtain several different-sized boxes, keeping in mind that students will handle them. Add weight to each box with sand, blocks, or other materials in varying amounts. Try to ensure that the size of a box isn't always relative to its weight—make some large boxes light and some small ones heavy. Seal each box and wrap it in brown mailing paper. For a more realistic touch, address the boxes. Then put them in the post office center with balance scales and postal scales.

Invite a pair of postal workers to estimate a package's weight and then weigh it on the postal scale. Have the students find another package they estimate to have the same weight and place both on a balance scale. Direct them to continue in this manner until they've weighed all the boxes. Encourage the pair to compare the boxes and then sort them by weight (heavy, medium, light) and by size (small, medium, large). Wow, wonder what's being mailed today?

Box	Weight	Price
⬜	1 oz.	5¢
⬜	2 oz.	7¢
⬜	3 oz.	9¢
⬜	4 oz.	10¢

Mystery Mail

Skills: *measuring weight, using money*

It's often easy to decide how much postage a letter needs. Since packages are mailed by weight, it's not as simple as putting a stamp on the box. Now that your little postal workers have some experience weighing packages, introduce them to charging postage by weight. Weigh several of the boxes from "Time to Weigh!" above and create a rate chart based on each box's weight. If desired, label each rate and the corresponding box with a different letter for easier matching. Encourage students in this center (customers) to take these packages to the post office to be mailed. Provide each customer with a coin purse filled with play money (or use copies of the coin patterns on page 63). At the post office, a worker weighs a package on the postal scale, checks the rate chart, and then charges the customer the appropriate amount of money. The customer pays the worker (and repeats the activity with a different package, if desired). Invite students to change roles so everyone has a turn.

On the Right Track
Skill: matching numerals

Postal workers need to know where mail is during the delivery process, and tracking numbers can help. A tracking number is assigned to a package. Then the sender and postal workers can track the package's whereabouts until it's delivered to the recipient.

Challenge your youngsters to track packages with this fun addition to your post office center. In advance, write a different series of three to six numerals on each of a set of packages. (Use the packages from "Time to Weigh!" on page 21.) Record the numbers on cards and place them in the post office. Next, hide the packages around the classroom. Explain to your group how tracking numbers work. Then invite a child in the center to read a number on a card, find the package with matching numerals, and then return the package to the post office for delivery. For more challenge, address several packages with locations in your classroom and have the student track and then deliver the mail.

Mail Call
Skills: writing numbers, understanding time, graphing

Once youngsters have some understanding of how the postal system uses plenty of math, why not use the system to reinforce some time-awareness and recording skills? In advance, duplicate the recording charts on page 25 to make a class supply. Also make a blank graph similar to the one shown and post it in your classroom. Help each child write a postcard to her family and address it to her home. Encourage her to pay special attention to the numbers in her street address and zip code. Next, provide each child with a postcard stamp. Walk with your class to the nearest mailbox to mail the postcards.

When you return to your classroom, give each child a recording chart and explain that she should take it home, check her mail, and color in one cell for each day her postcard does not arrive. When her card arrives, she should write an X in the appropriate cell and bring the sheet to school the next day. With the child's help, transfer the information from her recording chart to the class graph. When each child's information has been transferred, discuss and compare the data. When did the first postcard arrive? The last? After how many days were most postcards delivered?

Follow the Mail Trail

Cut.

Match.

Glue.

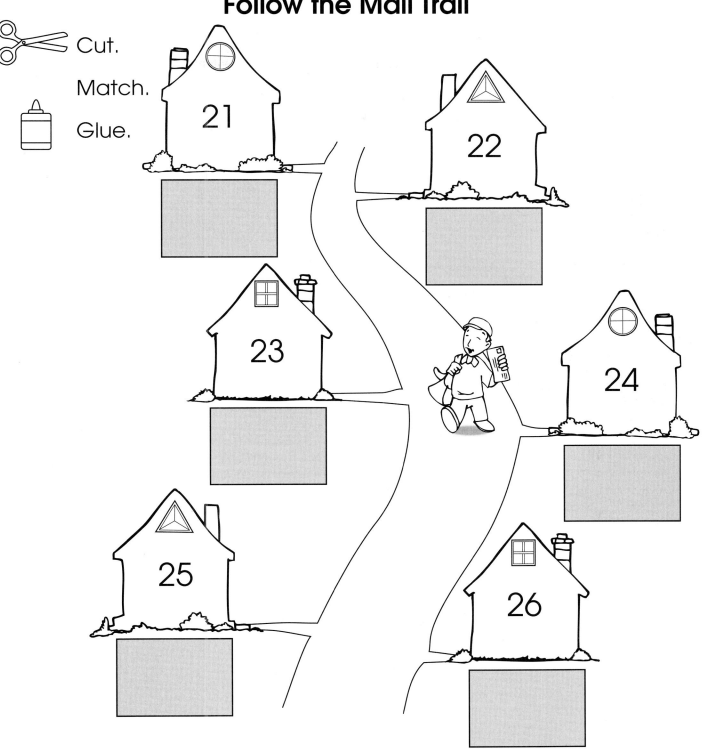

Bonus Box: On the back of this paper, draw your home. Write your address.

25   24   21   26   23   22

Stamp and Envelope Patterns

Use with "Stamp Champs" and "Postal Practice" on page 20.

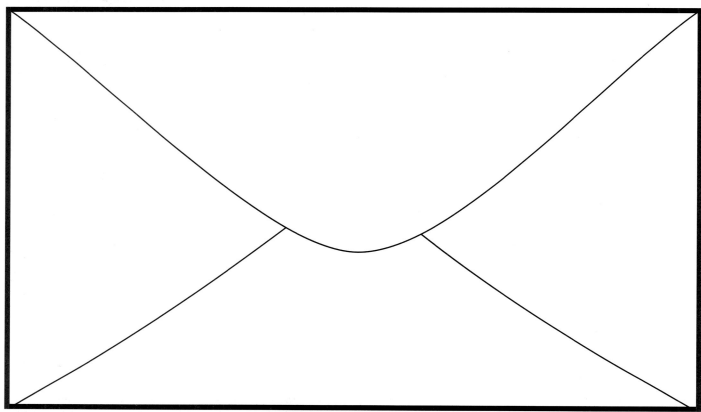

Name _____

I mailed my postcard on _____.

It arrived on _____.

1 day	2 days	3 days	4 days	5 days	6 days	7 days	8 days

©The Education Center, Inc. • *Out & About Math* • TEC3079

Name _____

I mailed my postcard on _____.

It arrived on _____.

1 day	2 days	3 days	4 days	5 days	6 days	7 days	8 days

©The Education Center, Inc. • *Out & About Math* • TEC3079

Out & About at the Movie Theater

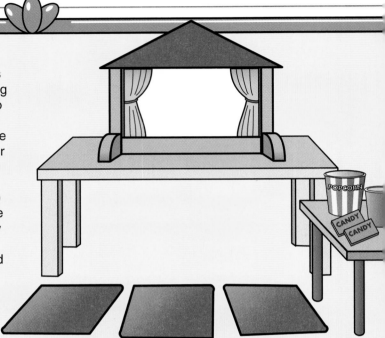

This magnificent movie theater study is sure to get rave reviews from your youngsters! The movie theater is chock-full of math skill reinforcement, from understanding what time the show begins to purchasing concessions to finding a seat in a specific row. Attending a matinee with your class can be an educational and fun field trip. These ideas are based upon an easy-to-set-up movie center for your classroom. Simply put a movie poster or sheet of white paper behind your puppet stage to resemble the movie screen. Place three rows of three chairs (or mats) each for the audience. Include a concession stand made from a small table and empty popcorn containers, candy boxes, and paper cups. The ticket booth can be easily made from a spare student desk with a roll of tickets and a shirt box decorated to resemble a cash register. For even more movie flair, add several old vests for usher uniforms. All set? Let's go!

It's Showtime!
Skill: *telling time to the hour*

When a person decides to go to the movies, she must know what time the show begins. The newspaper is often the first place people look for movie schedules. Photocopy the newspaper ad on page 30 for a small group. Store the copies in the movie center, along with a group supply of Judy clocks. Next, invite a small group to join you at the center. Explain that you want to see an afternoon movie and you need their help choosing one. Pass out a flyer and clock to each child. Encourage her to look at the first movie listing and then move her clock hands to match that time. Once you've made sure each student understands, move on to the next listing and have students match that time with their clocks. As a group, discuss the different times and determine whether the shows take place in the afternoon or evening. Continue in this manner until all the listings have been matched. Then choose a movie to attend together in your imaginations. Shh—it's starting!

Movie Munchies

Skills: *number recognition, understanding coin value, counting*

Not many of us can go to the movies and resist the treats at the concession stand. And the same will be true when your little ones see this scrumptious snack center! Add to your concession stand empty popcorn cartons and movie-candy boxes (or real treats, such as resealable snack bags of popcorn or mini packages of candy corn, jelly beans, M&M's candies, or Hershey's Kisses chocolates). Group the treats in baskets or shoeboxes according to size or type; then include price tags for coin values. Provide coin purses filled with various play coins (or use copies of the coin patterns on page 63). To use this center, one child acts as concession-stand cashier, and two or three others pretend to be movie patrons. Each patron chooses a treat, reads the price tag, and counts enough coins to pay the cashier. The cashier checks the amount and, if correct, gives the treat to the patron. For a greater challenge, encourage the patrons to pay with a coin of higher value so the cashier must make change.

Two Thumbs Up!

Skills: *tallying, graphing*

Movie theater managers must order concessions so that they have enough for busy times. They need to know what items are most popular with their customers in order to have enough supply to meet demand. Try this tallying and graphing activity to find out which items your concession stand should stock. Duplicate the tally sheet (page 31) to make a class supply. Also duplicate the snack cards (page 31) and place them in your concession stand. Use bulletin board paper and another copy of the snack cards to make a simple graph as shown. Distribute pencils and the tally sheets and demonstrate how to make a tally mark in the appropriate row when that treat is chosen. Next, have each child, in turn, walk to the concession stand and choose a snack pictured on one or more of the cards. Have her hold up the cards so the rest of the class can see them and then record her choices. (Remind each child to record her own choices.) When the tally sheets are complete, graph the findings. Post the completed graph in the concession stand and discuss the results. Lead your little movie managers to conclude which snack would require the most stock to be kept on hand.

We Like Movie Snacks!

Number of students (vertical axis, 1–20)

Types of snacks (horizontal axis): popcorn, soda, candy, nachos

Take Your Seats, Please

Skill: *estimating amounts*

Part of an usher's job is to help people find seats in the theater, so it really helps to be able to estimate how many people are in the theater and to know where any empty seats are located. To provide some movie estimation experience, place stuffed animals or dolls in some of your theater seats. Place small sheets of paper and pencils beside an empty box. Encourage each child to take a turn pretending to be the usher at the theater. Each child should estimate the number of movie patrons seated in the theater, write her name and estimate on a sheet of paper, and then put the sheet in the box. When everyone has taken a turn, gather the group and read the estimates. Together, count the number of patrons and determine the closest estimate. Afterward, discuss students' strategies for estimating. How many folks will come to the next showing?

Fresh, Hot, and Fun

Skills: *estimating, measuring, and comparing volume; counting*

Movies and popcorn are a perfect pair, but how much popcorn is best? This estimating and measuring activity is sure to please young movie patrons! In advance, fill a large tub or sensory table with air-popped popcorn. Place several dry-measuring cups and a small, medium, and large popcorn container (or plastic tumblers in three sizes) in the popcorn. Invite a pair of students to visit the center and estimate how many cups of popcorn will fill each container. Next, have the pair carefully measure the popcorn into each container, counting how many cups each holds. Then encourage the pair to compare the containers using vocabulary such as *more than* and *fewer than.* If desired, write a price on each container and invite students to determine the best value for the popcorn. As students leave the center, invite them to enjoy some fresh popcorn from a separate bowl!

At the Box Office

Ticket Prices

Babies = 1¢   Children = 5¢   Adults = 10¢

How much would it cost if the following people wanted to buy tickets together?

 Cut. Match. Glue.

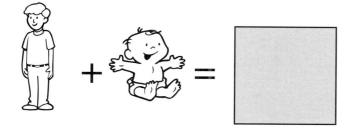

15¢   6¢   11¢   20¢   2¢   10¢

29

Movie Flyer
Use with "It's Showtime!" on page 26.

Now Showing at the Schoolhouse Movie Theater:

Fly Away Home

Shows at 1:00 4:00 7:00

Birdland

Shows at 2:00 5:00 8:00

PIXIE AND BOB

Shows at 3:00 7:00

Sunny Days

Shows at 4:00 8:00

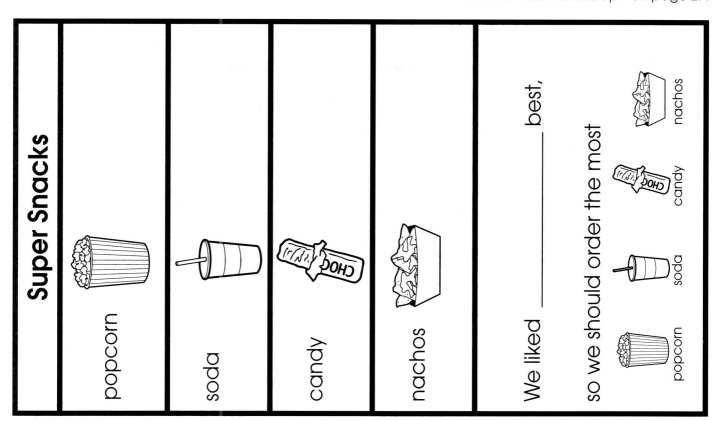

Super Snacks

popcorn

soda

candy

nachos

We liked _____ best,
so we should order the most

popcorn   soda   candy   nachos

popcorn   soda   candy   nachos

Out & About at the
Farm

Yee-ha! Get down and dirty with some everyday math on the farm! For a taste of the real thing, visit a local farm. Also set up a simple farm center in a sunny part of your classroom. If desired, cut out a barn shape from a flattened appliance box and enlist student help in painting on the appropriate shapes as shown. Round up some toy barnyard animals. Next, fill some large, shallow plastic storage boxes with moist potting soil to create fields. Collect packets of vegetable and fruit seeds. Then complete the center with some bandannas for costumes. All set? Let's go!

Creating Crops
Skills: *one-to-one correspondence, counting, tallying*

These days, crop planting is often done by machines, but years ago, farmers practiced lots of one-to-one correspondence when planting fields. Using a shallow plastic box filled with potting soil, demonstrate to students how to plant a seed by poking a hole in the soil, dropping in one vegetable seed (such as a lima bean), and covering it. Then give each child in a small group an opportunity to try her hand at planting a row of crops. Encourage her to whisper, "One hole, one seed" as she works. When the box is planted, help students water and care for the seeds. If desired, add more math skill practice by placing a small chalkboard or tablet nearby. As a class, observe the seeds and make a tally mark for each day that passes until the seeds sprout.

A Bumper Crop!
Skills: *sorting by attributes, size seriation, counting*

Reinforce plenty of math skills with this "veggie" interesting activity. Ask parents to donate a variety of fresh vegetables; then put them in the farm center. Explain to each small group, in turn, that many farmers inspect their produce to make sure it's good to eat. Next, have the children pretend to be farmers inspecting the produce. Help them sort the veggies by one attribute, such as small or not small. Then encourage each child to sort the veggies another way. For more skill enhancement, have students seriate, count, and compare the vegetables. Will everything make it to market?

Fresh From the Farm

Skills: measuring weight, using money

Many areas boast terrific farmers markets where local growers sell their fresh produce directly to customers. Reinforce measurement and money skills by using the leftover veggies from "A Bumper Crop!" on page 32 to create a market in your farm center. In advance, place in the center a scale, some paper lunch bags, and several coin purses filled with play money (or use copies of the reproducible on page 63). Have students help you create a price list similar to the one shown; then demonstrate to your class how to weigh and sell produce. Invite a small group to visit the market and take turns pretending to be customers and farmers. Rotate groups until each child has had a turn. Mmm—fresh veggies tonight!

corn	10¢ each
peas	20¢ a pound
carrots	20¢ each
tomatoes	10¢ each

"Egg-cellent" Farmers

Skills: sorting, one-to-one correspondence

Raising chickens means collecting and sorting the just-laid eggs. Try this Grade A activity to introduce youngsters to egg gathering. In advance, obtain a supply of white and brown plastic eggs and several clean, empty foam egg cartons. Then, while students are away from the classroom, place the eggs in low spots and on the floor. When students return, welcome them to the henhouse and have them gather all the eggs they can find and then bring them to a circle time. As a class, sort the eggs into white and brown groups and discuss the results. Compare the eggs using vocabulary such as *more than, fewer than,* and *equal to.* Then invite students to use one-to-one correspondence to fill the egg cartons in preparation for taking the eggs to market. Store the cartons in the farm center and encourage students to take turns re-sorting and counting the eggs.

Tip: If you can't find brown plastic eggs, simply fill white plastic eggs with sand (to weigh them), then soak them in a very strong tea solution for several days or until they are the desired shade.

33

Adding Animals
Skill: addition

Farmers take regular head counts of their livestock to make sure it's all safe and sound. Invite youngsters to pretend to be farm animals while adding down-home fun to circle time! In advance, make a class supply of the farm animal patterns on page 38 and cut the items apart. Give one animal pattern to each student and encourage him to color it and cut it out. Help each child tape his pattern to a paper strip; then fit the headband to his head and tape it in place. Invite students to wear their headbands to a circle time; then pretend to be a farmer describing her livestock. Call on various students to join you in the circle. Count the animals on their headbands and then say "I have [four] horses and [three] cows on my farm. How many animals do I have?" Help the seated students count and add the groups. Then have the "animals" sit down, and repeat the activity with different students. Continue gathering in this manner until each child has had a turn to pretend to be an animal.

Feeding on the Farm
Skills: measuring weight, comparing amounts

Farm animals eat plenty of oats and other grains. The larger the animal, the more food it will need. Give your little farmhands feeding time experience with this measurement activity. In advance, place a balance scale and several different toy farm animals (such as a pig, sheep, horse, and chicken) in the farm center. Fill a matching number of resealable plastic bags with different amounts of uncooked oatmeal; then seal the bags and tape them shut. Store them in the center in a silo (the oatmeal canister covered in red or silver paper). To complete the activity, a child looks at the animals and decides how much food each will eat based on its size. Then she opens the silo and removes the bags. She visually compares the bags and then compares them by weighing pairs of bags on the balance scale. Then she matches the bags with the appropriate animals. It's chow time!

Corresponding Cattle
Skill: matching numerals

It's roundup time! Help your farmhands round up some stray cattle with this numeral-matching activity. To prepare, make a class supply of paper circles. Program each with a different number from 0 to 20 and add a small roll of masking tape to the back of each. Also make several lists of six numbers apiece. During a circle time, choose three or four student volunteers to be farmhands and give each a number list. Then have the rest of the class pretend to be cows, and give each child a number circle. Direct him to tape his number to his shirt over his tummy and then slowly roam around the room while the farmhands round up the numbers on their lists. If desired, when the farmhands have found all their cattle, repeat with a new set of farmhands.

Mending Fences
Skills: comparing sizes and shapes of plane figures

What shape makes the best animal pen? This center activity will help students find out. In advance, put 12 identical rectangular blocks in your farm center. Also include a supply of plastic toy farm animals, a set of shape pictures (for student reference), sticky notes, and a pencil. To use this center, a student uses all 12 blocks to build a fence in a geometric shape. Next, he puts all the farm animals inside it and decides whether the animals have enough room to move around comfortably and safely. Then he uses all the blocks to build a different geometric fence and checks the amount of room again. He continues in this manner until he has made a circle, square, triangle, and rectangle from the blocks; then he chooses the shape that made the best fence. He draws that shape on a sticky note and adds his initials. He puts the sticky note in a predetermined location and then cleans up the area for the next student. When each child has had a turn building fences, draw a simple graph on your chalkboard and have students use their sticky notes to graph their preferences.

Farmer Bob's Morning

Farmer Bob has chores to do. Help him get them done on time.

 Color. Cut. Match. Glue.

| 5:00 | 7:00 | 8:00 | 9:00 | 6:00 | 10:00 |

Hay Is for Horses

It's feeding time!

 Color. Cut. Match. Glue.

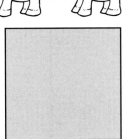

©The Education Center, Inc. • *Out & About Math* • TEC3079

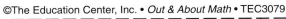

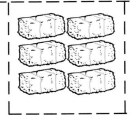 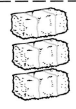 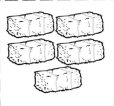 

Out & About at the
Ice-Cream Parlor

Ice-cream parlors are a staple of many a childhood, so it makes sense to learn about the math involved in getting a tasty treat. If possible, take your class on a mini field trip to a nearby ice-cream parlor to observe real-life math in action. Also set up an ice-cream-parlor center in your classroom with an order counter and a table with chairs. Make several batches of different-colored play dough and store them behind the counter with some plastic ice-cream scoops. Include abstract shapes cut from tan and dark brown craft foam to represent caramel and fudge toppings. Place portions of cotton batting in a whipped topping container to represent whipped cream. Fill an empty plastic jar with red pom-poms to represent cherries. Add a supply of cone-shaped paper drinking cups to serve as ice-cream cones and some disposable plastic bowls and spoons for making sundaes. If desired, add some aprons for the parlor staff. Don't forget a cash register (lidded box) stocked with play money or copies of the reproducible on page 63. All set? Let's go!

Ice-Cream Treats	
1-scoop cone	5¢
2-scoop cone	7¢
Sundae	10¢
Extra cherries	1¢ each
Extra whipped cream	2¢

Playing and Paying at the Parlor

Skills: coin recognition, understanding coin values

Here's an activity that will prompt your little ones to use real coins to buy imitation ice cream! As a class, discuss the treats and prices found in a real ice-cream shop. Together, make a menu poster similar to the one shown; then post it in the ice-cream-parlor center. Finally, review the value and appearance of pennies, nickels, and dimes; then add several small, stocked coin purses to the center. (You can also substitute play coins or copies of the reproducible on page 63.)

To use this center, have a small group of children pretend to order cones, cups, and sundaes from the menu and then pay with the appropriate coins. Encourage two children to pretend to be workers who assemble the ice-cream treats and add up the orders. Who knew practicing money skills could be so deliciously fun?

Scoop Subtraction
Skills: counting, subtraction

For more fun in the ice-cream parlor, have youngsters pretend to be ice-cream servers selling scoops. To prepare, place 10 same-colored play dough balls (ice-cream scoops) in a clean, empty ice-cream carton. Then make four to six cards, each labeled with a numeral from 0 to 4, and place them facedown on a table. Working with one small group at a time, explain that you are pretending to be an ice-cream parlor owner trying out a new flavor to see whether it sells. Explain that the students are workers who will be selling the scoops at the parlor. Pass the container to one child and have her draw a number card from the pile on the table. Explain that the number on the card represents the number of scoops she sold. Have her remove the corresponding number of scoops from the carton. Then count together with the group the number of scoops that are left in the carton. Continue until everyone has had a turn to "sell" scoops from the carton. How many scoops are left? Was the flavor popular? Should you continue to sell it in the ice-cream parlor?

Favorite Flavors
Skills: surveying, tallying, counting

Everyone has a favorite flavor of ice cream! Encourage your students to find out some favorites as they conduct a survey. Give each child a copy of the survey sheet on page 44. Ask him to choose three flavors of ice cream; then have him color the three scoops on the survey to resemble those flavors. Have him write or dictate the flavor names below the scoops. Then ask him to survey ten students and ask their preference among the three flavors. Have him use tally marks to record students' answers. Then have him count the tally marks in each column and write the corresponding numeral at the bottom of the column. At a group time, have each child share the results of his survey with the class.

Rhett 's Ice-Cream Survey		
Cherry	butter pecan	chocolate
I	IIII I	III I
1	5	4

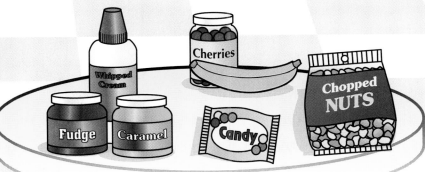

All Sorts of Toppings

Skill: *sorting*

Bring in some ice-cream toppings to give your youngsters practice with sorting. Gather a small group of students around a table and show them jars of hot fudge and caramel, a jar of cherries, a can of whipped cream, a package of candies, a package of chopped nuts, and a banana. Tell youngsters that a coworker in their ice-cream parlor unloaded the sundae supplies but didn't sort them first, so now it's hard to tell customers what's available. Next, ask them to sort the toppings into categories: sauces, candy, etc. Then ask them to sort the toppings a different way. Which toppings are usually served hot? Cold? Room temperature? Or ask youngsters to sort the toppings into the categories of liquid and solid.

When the sorting is over, use the toppings with "Sundae Sequence" on page 42.

Scoop After Scoop

Skills: *estimating amounts, counting*

How many scoops are in a gallon of ice cream? Ice-cream-parlor managers must know how far a gallon will go in order to keep enough on hand for hungry customers. Pretend to be a manager and have students pretend to be workers during this estimation activity to discover the scoop on scoops! Show the class a gallon container of vanilla ice cream and an ice-cream scoop. Ask each child to estimate how many scoops you will be able to get from the container. Have her record her estimate on a sticky note, along with her name. Then start scooping! Put each scoop in a separate disposable plastic bowl. (Periodically ask an assistant to take the bowls to a freezer so that the ice cream won't melt before using in "Sundae Sequence" on page 42.) Have students count as you scoop to determine the actual number of scoops. Then have students review their estimates to see who was closest to the actual number.

Tip: A gallon of ice cream contains approximately 42 average-sized scoops.

41

Sundae Sequence
Skills: sequencing ordinal numbers

Check with families for food allergies; then use the scoops of ice cream from "Scoop After Scoop" on page 41, as well as the toppings from "All Sorts of Toppings" on page 41, for some mouthwatering math! Working with one small group at a time, give each child a copy of the sequencing pictures on page 45 and a 4" x 18" strip of construction paper. Ask each child to color the pictures and cut them apart. Have her glue the pictures to her construction paper strip to reflect her chosen sequence for building an ice-cream sundae. (She may choose not to use all of the pictures.) Then have her take her sequence strip to a table where you have set up the toppings. Give her a bowl with a scoop of ice cream; then have her follow the sequence she has designed for making her sundae. As students enjoy their creations, have them explain to their tablemates the order they chose for their sundae building. Did anyone build a sundae in the same order?

Melting Away
Skills: estimating and measuring time

All good things must come to an end—even a scoop of ice cream! But how long does it take for a scoop of the cold creamy stuff to melt? Find out with this activity! Explain the experiment to your students: You'll be placing a scoop of ice cream in a disposable plastic bowl on a table in your classroom. Ask each child to record on a sticky note the number of minutes she thinks will pass before the ice cream is completely melted. Then scoop out the ice cream and time it to see how long it takes to melt. Have each child check her estimate. Who was closest to the actual melting time? Discuss the results and lead students to conclude that ice cream is best stored in freezers so it will stay frozen and good to eat.

Selling Scoops

Mary and Harry work at the ice-cream parlor. Who sold more cones each day?

Count.

✓ Make a check mark.

Who sold more?

	Mary			Harry
Monday	🍦🍦🍦🍦			🍦🍦🍦🍦🍦🍦
Tuesday	🍦🍦🍦🍦🍦🍦🍦			🍦🍦🍦🍦🍦🍦
Wednesday	🍦🍦🍦🍦🍦🍦			🍦🍦🍦🍦
Thursday	🍦🍦🍦🍦🍦			🍦🍦🍦🍦🍦🍦🍦🍦
Friday	🍦🍦🍦🍦🍦🍦🍦🍦			🍦🍦🍦🍦🍦🍦🍦🍦

Bonus Box: Use cubes or another manipulative to figure out how many cones Mary and Harry sold all together on each day.

_____'s Ice-Cream Survey

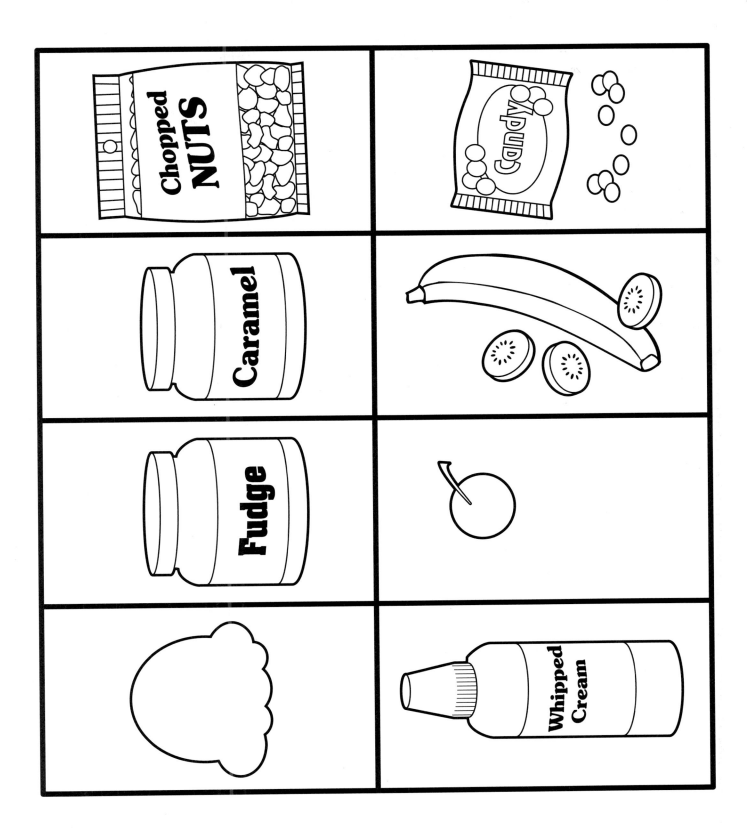

Out & About at the
Pizza Place

Neighborhood pizza restaurants are known as family-friendly places, so it's likely that many students have visited one. As an added bonus to the delicious pizza, these restaurants rely on plenty of math. If possible, take your students for a slice at a nearby pizza restaurant. Also set up a pizza place in your classroom. Begin with a long, low table for a kitchen counter and include spatulas, oven mitts, pizza pans (or cardboard cake circles), aprons, and craft-foam pizza ingredients. Cut tan foam wedges of crust to fit the pizza pans. Next, cut red foam sauce to fit the wedges. Also cut foam green peppers, mushrooms, pepperoni slices, sausage crumbles, and ham. Onions and shredded cheese are easily simulated with yarn bits or more craft foam. Store the ingredients in plastic, lidded containers and encourage students to keep the ingredients sorted. On one end of the counter, set up a cash register (lidded box) with some play money or copies of the coin patterns on page 63. Also set up a dining area with a small table and chairs. Photocopy the pizza menu/order form on page 51 to make a supply; then store the copies in the dining area with several pencils. Put paper plates and napkins in the dining area, along with a supply of plastic cups. All set? Let's go!

Order Up!

Skills: *using one-to-one correspondence, counting*

It's lunchtime at the pizza place, and things are hopping! Invite each small group of students, in turn, to enjoy some math and dramatic play at the pizza place. Give each child several play coins (or copies of the reproducible on page 63). Then invite one child to be the server and seat a group of three or four customers. Encourage another child to act as chef and wait behind the counter for the order. Have the server use one-to-one correspondence to give each customer a napkin, cup, and plate. Direct the customers to look over the order form together and decide on their pizza preferences. Next, have the server take the customers' order (using a copy of the form on page 51) and deliver it to the chef, who will make their pizza with the foam pieces and let the server know when it's ready for the table. The server must make sure the order is accurate and then serve the customers. The customers will then check their order, enjoy some play pizza, and pay their bill. Don't forget the tip!

That's How It's Made!

Skills: sequencing, counting, measuring time

Mama Mia! How do you make such excellent pizza? By carefully following sequenced directions, of course! In advance, create a set of simply illustrated cards, each showing a different step for making pizza. Place the cards in the pizza kitchen along with a kitchen timer. To complete this activity, a student pretends to be a pizza chef and sequences the cards. Next, she makes a pizza accordingly. She sets the timer and "bakes" her pizza for the required amount of time. Then she pretends to serve it to customers.

To vary this activity, add more cards depicting different types and amounts of pizza toppings. If desired, make additional sets of recipe cards showing how to make different types of pizza from start to finish; then bind each set to make separate booklets. Store booklets in the pizza place center. When the chef receives a customer's order, have her locate the card set that matches the order form and then follow that sequence to make the pizza. Smells good—is it ready yet?

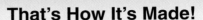

More Cheese, Please!

Skills: following a sequence, comparing sets

Here's a small-group activity guaranteed to bring plenty of pizza preparation fun! In advance, make several different sets of pizza recipe cards, or use the ones prepared in "That's How It's Made!" above. Invite a group of four students to join you at the pizza place; then show the students the foam pizza ingredients and sets of cards. Pair students and then give each a set of cards. Next, direct the students to make a pizza according to their card sequence. When the pizzas are ready, have the students compare them and discuss the results. Which ingredients are alike? Which are different? Encourage students to use the terms *more, fewer,* and *equal* when describing the pizzas. Repeat the activity with different card sets and then with different groups of students.

Speedy Delivery

Skills: counting, estimating time, measuring time

Does it take longer to bake a pizza with one topping or one with everything on it? Chefs need to know cooking times so that orders can go out together. Here's a tasty and timely experiment for your little chefs. In advance, purchase one English muffin for every two students. Also prepare pizza sauce, cheese, and three different kinds of toppings. Place each ingredient in a separate bowl (with a spoon) on a table and then label each bowl as shown. Use a permanent marker to personalize a five-inch square of aluminum foil for each child. Have four cookie sheets nearby for easy transfer—one for each number of available toppings.

Have each student, in turn, wash her hands, place a muffin half on her sheet of foil, and then carefully prepare the pizza of her choice. At the end of your assembly line, help each child place her pizza on a baking sheet as shown. Ask students whether it will take longer for a plain cheese pizza to bake than one with extra toppings. Next, invite each child to estimate how many minutes each group of pizzas should bake in order to melt the cheese. Record each estimate on a chart. Have an adult helper bake the pizzas with the help of a pair of student timekeepers. Instruct the timekeepers to use a stopwatch to count the minutes while the pizzas bake. Before serving the baked pizzas, compare the students' estimates with the actual baking times and discuss the results. Okay—time to eat!

Popular Pizza

Skills: graphing

After enjoying the personalized pizzas made in "Speedy Delivery" above, illustrate students' favorite toppings with this set of graphs. For each topping, prepare a simple graph as shown. Place a supply of sticky notes and pencils near each graph. As each student finishes eating his pizza, read aloud the choices and explain that the "No, thank you" column is for students who didn't wish to try that particular topping. Then invite each child to graph how he liked each of his pizza toppings. To do this, he goes to each graph, in turn, and writes his initials on a sticky note. He puts his note in the appropriate column and moves to the next graph. When each child has completed every graph, discuss the results. Have students compare the results on individual graphs and then compare among graphs. What's the class favorite?

Ham		
I like it.	I do not like it.	No, thank you.
AS	AW	SM
JA	JM	DL
MP	XW	KW
JC		KB
KH		MS
TJ		SS

Name _____

Pizza Shapes

✂ Cut. Match. 🍶 Glue.

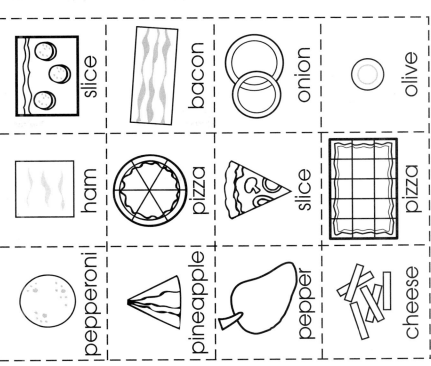

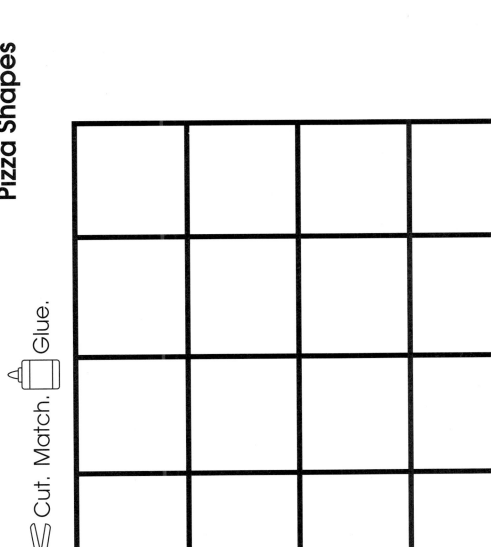

Name_____

The Best Pizza

Which pizza toppings does your family like?
Make a tally mark for each person's choice.

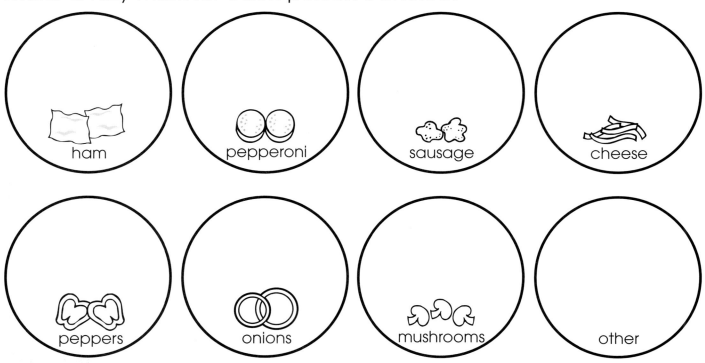

Color one box for each tally mark to graph the choices.

Family Favorites

Type of Toppings	1	2	3	4	5	6	7	8
ham								
pepperoni								
sausage								
cheese								
peppers								
onions								
mushrooms								
other								

Number of People Who Like These Toppings

©The Education Center, Inc. • *Out & About Math* • TEC3079

May I Take Your Order?

 Pizza 10¢

 Toppings 1¢ each

 Pick.

 ham _____ 1¢

 mushrooms _____ 1¢

 sausage _____ 1¢

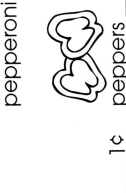 pepperoni _____ 1¢

 peppers _____ 1¢

 onions _____ 1¢

How many toppings? _____

Add. 10¢ + _____ ¢ = _____ ¢

May I Take Your Order?

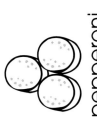 Pizza 10¢

Toppings 1¢ each

Pick.

ham _____ 1¢

mushrooms _____ 1¢

sausage _____ 1¢

 pepperoni _____ 1¢

peppers _____ 1¢

 onions _____ 1¢

How many toppings? _____

Add. 10¢ + _____ ¢ = _____ ¢

Out & About at the

Garden Center

Math skills are always in full bloom at the garden center! If possible, take your students to visit a nearby center. Discuss students' experiences in garden centers, from plant nurseries to centers included in home-improvement or discount stores. Also set up a garden center in your classroom. Begin with a supply of various sizes of plastic flowerpots and matching saucers. Add shopping baskets, a large supply of silk flowers and greenery, some Styrofoam blocks or florist's foam, and plastic, child-safe garden tools. Also add a quantity of herb and flower seed packets, making sure to obtain varying numbers of each type of flower or herb. If desired, include sealed bags of "fertilizer" and "mulch" (scrap paper). Be sure to set up a cash register (lidded box) with some play money or copies of the coin patterns on page 63. All set? Let's go!

Seed Packet Sorting

Skills: sorting, counting, comparing sets

Before planting a garden, you've got to know what kinds of seeds you want. Cultivate lots of math skills with this simple sorting activity! Ask a pair or small group of youngsters to sort the supply of flower and herb packets. For a very simple sort, have students group the flower seeds and the herb seeds. Or ask students to sort the packets by type of flower or herb (zinnias, marigolds, basil, etc.). When they have finished sorting, ask youngsters to count the number of packets in each group. Ask questions to help them compare the groups, using the terms *most, fewest,* and *equal.*

Packet Problems
Skill: sorting

Use seed packets again to put your students' problem-solving skills to work! Direct each small group of students, in turn, to examine the backs of the seed packets. Point out the basic planting information shown there, such as how many days the seeds might take to germinate, how tall the plants will grow, and whether the plants like sun or shade. (If your packets do not have easy-to-read icons, consider drawing them with permanent marker.) Then give the group a collection of seed packets. Pose one of the following problems; then ask the group to sort the seed packets appropriately.

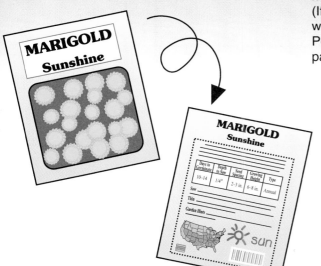

- You want to plant a garden with all [red] and [pink] flowers. Which seeds should you choose?
- You want all the flowers in your garden to grow to at least one foot in height. Which seeds should you choose?
- Your garden area is very sunny. Which seeds should you choose?
- You want all the flowers in your garden to bloom during the summer. Which seeds should you choose?

Herb Gardens on a Budget
Skills: coin recognition, using money

Your young gardeners will have to dig into their pockets to pay for packets in this activity which focuses on money skills. Put a sticky dot on each herb seed packet. On each sticky dot, write "5¢" or "10¢." Then give each child in a small group 30 cents in nickels and dimes. Explain that each child has a 30-cent budget to buy the seeds needed to start an herb garden. Ask each child, in turn, to select the herb seeds he'd like to buy with his coins. On a sheet of paper, record the type of herb, number of packets, and cost. Then have him pay you with his coins. Give him any needed change and a copy of the written receipt. Then invite the next customer to select and pay for the herbs of her choice.

Heavy, Heavier, Heaviest!
Skills: estimating and measuring weight

Don't "weight"—try this measurement activity today! To prepare, put three different amounts of potting soil (one-half pound, one pound, and two pounds) into three resealable plastic bags. Seal the bags and, if desired, tape the seals to prevent spills. Set the three bags on a table in the garden center, along with a small scale.

To introduce this center, show youngsters a small bag of potting soil from a garden center. Explain that soil is sold in bags of varying weights to accommodate different planting projects. Then tell your students that at this center, they'll estimate the weight of the potting soil in the plastic bags. A child lifts each bag and then moves the bags around to place them in order from lightest to heaviest. She then weighs each bag on the scale to determine whether the order is correct.

Fill 'em Up!
Skills: estimating and measuring volume

Of course, once you've bought a bag of potting soil, you have to put it into pots to see how far it goes! So after your students explore weight, invite them to explore volume with this activity. To prepare, cover the floor area in the center to keep things neat. Then fill a large tub with potting soil or sand. Provide a few different sizes of flowerpots and one or two measuring cups. Have a child estimate how many cups of soil or sand it will take to fill one of the pots. Then have him use a measuring cup to check his estimate. Have him continue by estimating and checking the volume of a different flowerpot. When he's all done filling the pots, remind him to dump the soil or sand back into the tub for the next gardener to use!

Color Combinations
Skill: addition

Plant an understanding of simple addition with this flowery idea! To begin, give a child a rectangle of Styrofoam packing material or florist's foam to use as a planter, five red silk flowers, five yellow silk flowers, and a copy of the recording sheet on page 58. Ask her to plant the flowers in the planter (stick the stems into the foam) in all the possible combinations of five flowers. Have her color in the flowers on the recording sheet to show each combination she discovers. Let's see…two red plus three yellow equals five!

Stepping Stones
Skills: estimating, counting, and comparing amounts, using nonstandard measurement

Nothing finishes a garden like a path of stepping stones! But how many do you need? Challenge youngsters to estimate the number of paper stepping stones they'll need to complete a path in your classroom. To begin, use masking tape to mark off a path on the floor. For example, you might mark off a path from your garden center area to the door. Show students a stepping stone purchased at your local garden center. Then show them some paper "stones" you've made by tracing around the real stone. Ask them to estimate how many of the stones will be needed to complete the path marked by the tape line. Remind them that a small amount of space will be left between the stones. Place two or three stones in a line to demonstrate and help them estimate. Record each child's estimate. Then have volunteers put the paper stones along the path. Count the actual number and compare it to your students' estimates.

To enhance the activity, tape off one or two other paths in or around your classroom. Have students compare the number of stones needed to complete each path.

Name_____

An Orderly Garden

✂ Cut.
🧴 Match.
✏ Glue.
✏ Write.

one	two	three	four	five

Name

The Long and Short of Tools

Cut out the tools.

Glue them in order from longest to shortest.

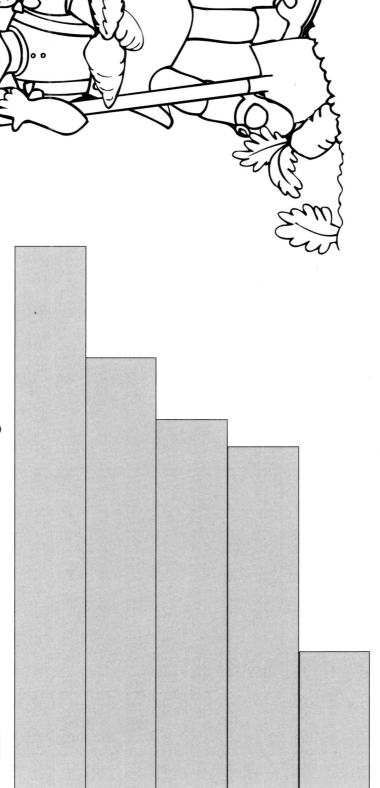

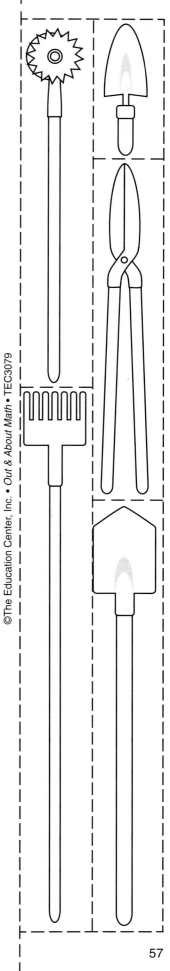

Recording Sheet

Use with "Color Combinations" on page 55.

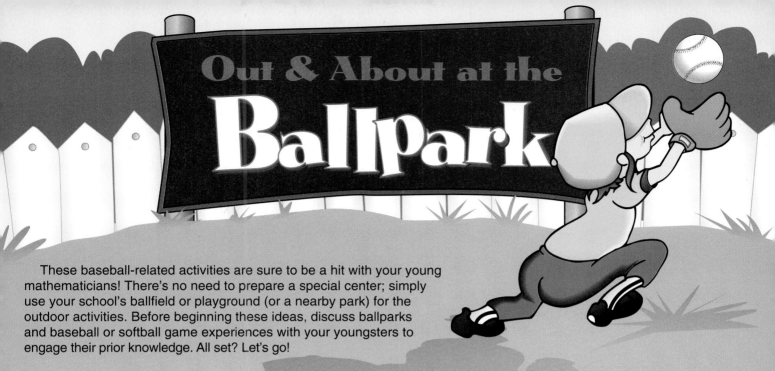

Out & About at the Ballpark

These baseball-related activities are sure to be a hit with your young mathematicians! There's no need to prepare a special center; simply use your school's ballfield or playground (or a nearby park) for the outdoor activities. Before beginning these ideas, discuss ballparks and baseball or softball game experiences with your youngsters to engage their prior knowledge. All set? Let's go!

Keeping Score

Skills: ordinal numbers, number recognition, addition

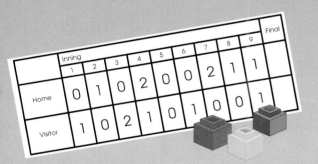

A good baseball fan should know how to read the scoreboard! Duplicate the simple scoreboard on page 62 once for each small group in your class. Show a copy of the scoreboard to one small group at a time; then ask each child to answer questions about it, such as the following:

* How many runs did the home team score in the fifth inning?
* How many runs did the visiting team score in the third inning?
* Did the home team get any runs in the eighth inning?

After asking each child to answer questions related to the scoreboard, ask the group to cooperatively add up the scores for each of the teams. (Provide Unifix cubes or other manipulatives to help students.) Write the sums in the final score column. Who won the game?

Team by the Numbers

Skill: number order

The roster for the team lists the players in numerical order—3, 4, 7, 10. Give youngsters practice with ordering numbers as they put their own team in order! Write nine different numbers (between 0 and 20) on individual sheets of white copy paper. Then tape one number sheet to the back of each of nine students' shirts. Have the students represent ball players and stand in front of the group so that their numbers are visible. Then ask students to put this ball team in order! Have student volunteers move each player into place so that the nine numbers are in order from smallest to largest, left to right. Repeat the activity at another time, using different numbers and allowing nine different students to be the ball players.

Run, Run, As Fast As You Can!

Skills: estimating and measuring time

Get out a stopwatch and see just how fast your base runners are! In your outdoor play area, mark off 60 feet, the same length between two bases in a Little League game. Ask each child to estimate how many seconds it will take her to run this distance. Have students record their names and estimates on sticky notes. Then have each child, in turn, run the distance as you time her with a stopwatch. Was her estimate close? Whose was closest?

If you have an area large enough, mark off all four bases, with 60 feet between every two bases. Have students estimate how long it will take them to run all the bases.

"Stee-rike"!

Skills: counting, tallying

Will the count be loaded when your young pitchers step onto the mound? Try this partner activity and see! To prepare, duplicate the balls and strikes chart on page 62 for each child. Have a student lie down on top of a long length of bulletin board paper while you outline his body with a marker. Next, use a different color of marker to outline the strike zone on the body outline as shown. Post the body outline on a wall, with the feet at floor level.

Invite one pair of students at a time to try the activity. One child is the pitcher and one is the umpire. The pitcher stands several feet away and throws a yarn ball toward the body outline (the batter), trying to hit inside the strike zone. If he does, the umpire makes a tally mark in the "Strikes" column. If the pitcher misses the strike zone, the umpire makes a tally mark in the "Balls" column. Each pitcher gets six pitches to try to strike out the batter. Then the partners review the count of balls and strikes before switching roles and filling out a new chart for the new pitcher.

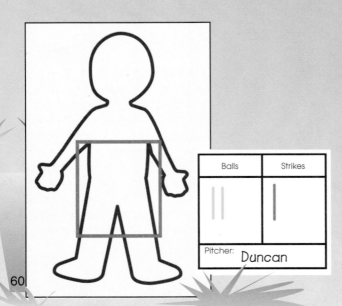

Park Problems

Skills: telling time to the hour

Have students use individual Judy clocks (or another manipulative clock) to help them solve these game-time problems!

- The ball game starts at 2:00 and lasts about two hours. What time will it be over?
- Your game starts at 1:00, but you have to be at the park one hour early for batting practice. What time should you arrive at the park?
- Practice starts at 5:00 and ends at 7:00. How many hours will it be?
- Today you have a doubleheader. The first game starts at 3:00 and lasts about two hours. What time will it be over? Then the second game begins one hour later. What time will it start?

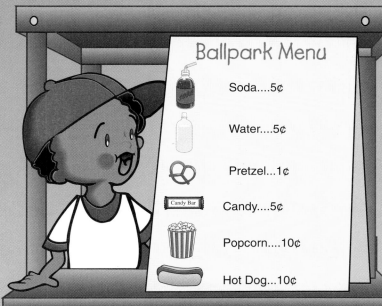

Ballpark Menu

Soda....5¢

Water....5¢

Pretzel...1¢

Candy....5¢

Popcorn....10¢

Hot Dog...10¢

At the Concession Stand

Skills: coin recognition, understanding coin values

Of course, no baseball game is complete without some ballpark snacks! Make up a simple menu similar to the one shown. Working with one small group at a time, give each child several play pennies, nickels, and dimes. (Or use copies of the coin patterns on page 63.) Invite each child to order the snacks of his choice from the menu and pay you with his coins. Does he get change? If there are no food allergies or sensitivities among your students, reward their efforts with a *real* ballpark favorite: Cracker Jack popcorn!

Scoreboard
Use with "Keeping Score" on page 59.

Inning	1	2	3	4	5	6	7	8	9	Final
Home	0	1	0	2	0	0	2	1	1	
Visitor	1	0	2	1	0	1	0	0	1	

Balls and Strikes Chart
Use with "'Stee-rike'!" on page 60.

Balls	Strikes	Balls	Strikes

Pitcher:

Pitcher:

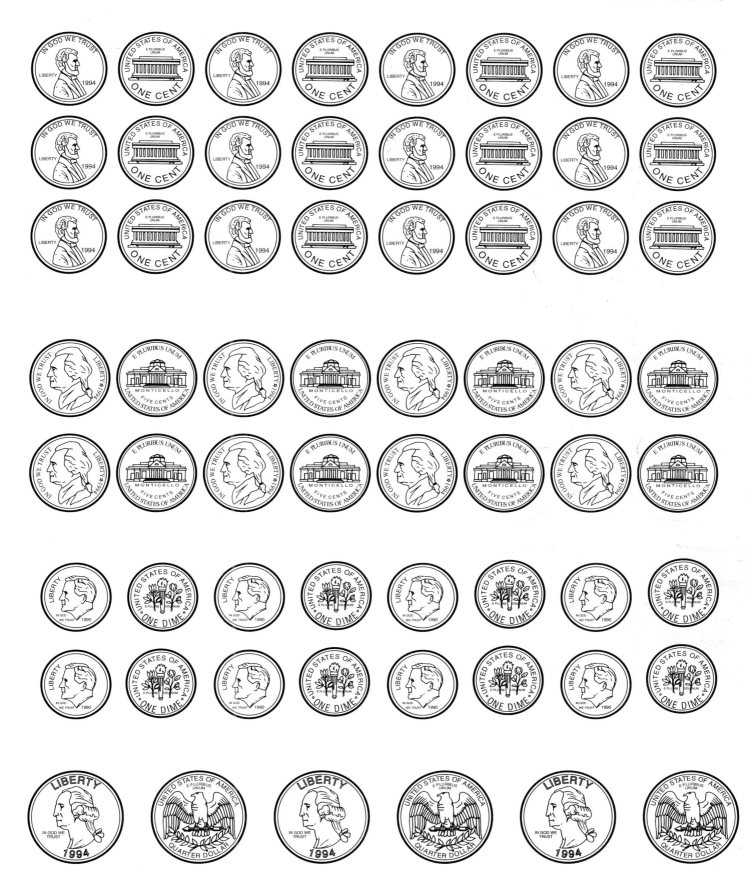

Managing Editor: Allison E. Ward

Editor at Large: Diane Badden

Contributing Writers: Randi Austin, Ada Goren, Melissa Hauck, Alison LaManna

Copy Editors: Sylvan Allen, Karen Brewer Grossman, Amy Kirtley-Hill, Karen L. Huffman, Debbie Shoffner

Cover Artists: Nick Greenwood, Clint Moore

Art Coordinator: Nick Greenwood

Artists: Pam Crane, Clevell Harris, Ivy L. Koonce, Sheila Krill, Clint Moore, Greg D. Rieves, Rebecca Saunders, Barry Slate

Typesetters: Lynette Dickerson, Mark Rainey

President, The Mailbox Book Company™: Joseph C. Bucci

Director of Book Planning and Development: Chris Poindexter

Book Development Managers: Cayce Guiliano, Thad McLaurin, Susan Walker

Curriculum Director: Karen P. Shelton

Editorial Research Manager: Elizabeth H. Linsday

Traffic Manager: Lisa K. Pitts

Librarian: Dorothy C. McKinney

Editorial and Freelance Management: Karen A. Brudnak

Editorial Training: Irving P. Crump

Editorial Assistants: Hope Rodgers, Jan E. Witcher

www.themailbox.com

©2003 by THE EDUCATION CENTER, INC.
All rights reserved.
ISBN# 1-56234-523-0

Manufactured in the United States
10 9 8 7 6 5 4 3 2 1